BITTERSWEET REVENGE

A true short story

Joseph C Amadi

To my family

Prologue

This is the true story of Nneka, an intelligent young girl who came from a poverty-stricken background in the small village community of Obodo-Ukwu in south-eastern Nigeria. Her father was a poor farmer, who could hardly make enough money to feed his wife and three children. Nneka had little hope of a rosy future; nonetheless, she was determined to turn her dreams of bettering herself into reality.

When Nneka went to live with her uncle and aunt in Lagos city, to work as a maid, she had high hopes of continuing her education when they promised to enrol her at college. She was soon prohibited from contacting her parents, and she was mistreated and not permitted to leave the house without her aunt's consent. She was treated like a slave, working around the clock every day and being subjected to sexual abuse by her uncle.

Nneka endured seven long years of mistreatment, prevarication and a dreadful waste of her talents at the hands of her uncle, Chief Uzodike, and his wife, Oluchi. Her hopes of a better life for herself and her family began to fade when she became pregnant by her uncle, who had initially promised her heaven and earth.

One

Nneka was the eldest daughter of her parent's three children. She came from a poverty-stricken background, her parents being unable to afford to send Nneka and her two siblings to school. Despite being such a brilliant and ambitious young teenager, who had a high ambition to become a teacher, Nneka ended up being a school dropout as a result of having no one to assist her to fulfil her true potential.

Nneka and her parents lived in an old dilapidated, two-bedroomed mud house in the remote shanty town of Obodo-Ukwu in south-eastern Nigeria. Her dad, Mr Anaeke aka Agwu-Turumbe was a peasant farmer and local palm wine tapper, and her mum, Mrs Rosemary, was a petty trader in the local village. Due to absolute poverty, the three children had to live on leftover food from the neighbourhood as their parents struggled to feed them.

Nneka and her family really made every effort to make ends meet as hardship and hunger were at their door, when news came from Chief Uzodike that he planned to visit the village in two weeks. He intended to take Nneka with him to his house in Lagos.

"I have just been told that my brother, Chief Uzodike, and his wife, Oluchi, will be visiting our house in two weeks' time," said Nneka's mum, Rosemary.

"Oh my God, who told you Mum? What a pleasant surprise! I can't wait to meet my uncle and his wife again," Nneka replied excitedly. "Mum, God has heard our prayers, it is great news! God is *so* wonderful. I haven't spoken to my uncle for ages. I feel pretty good and I am looking forward to seeing him soon. Mum, do you know that we will soon be getting out of poverty? It is only just a matter of time."

"Yes my daughter, Nneka, you are absolutely right, and I don't know what to say until my brother turns up."

Nneka and her parents were exhilarated, dancing and joyful whilst awaiting the arrival of her uncle and his wife.

"I know your uncle, Chief Uzodike, is a powerful, influential and God-fearing person, but he was not always easy to get along with. He loves women, is a womaniser, but there is a saying that charity begins at home," Anaeke said to Nneka in a jovial mood. "My daughter, Nneka, you know quite well that I tried all I could to see that you and your siblings attended school. I wanted you to learn how to read and write, so you could all achieve your full potential, but unfortunately it didn't work out as well for me as I had expected. I am hoping that your uncle will continue from where I stopped."

"Thank you, Dad, for all the efforts and the sacrifices you have made," Nneka replied. "Determination is the key to success and I believe that where there is life there is always hope. I hope in the near future this extreme indigent suffering and beleaguered condition of ours will soon be alleviated. I am going to fulfil every promise made and I am looking forward to the enormous challenges ahead of me."

"Nneka, my daughter, I believe in everything you say," her mum replied. "I do understand your empathy. I am quite aware of your expectations and know quite well that you are a clever and assiduous young girl, who is eager and anxious to uplift your family if any opportunity arises. However, I do believe whatever is inextricable there must be an indispensable solution."

***

As Nneka's motivated parents were making the final preparations for the arrival of her uncle and his wife, her irrepressible fastidious mum, Rosemary, wanted to ensure that her daughter was dressed smartly and looked like a city girl instead of an ugly village girl. Rosemary suggested the idea of trying to borrow some money to purchase all the most necessary items such as clothes, shoes, slippers, underwear, cosmetics and toiletries, which her daughter needed to travel with her uncle to the city. She knew quite well that it would be a difficult task to ask for money from her friends and neighbours.

Rosemary started her quest by visiting one of her grumpy neighbours, Mrs Oluchi, to ask her to lend her some money.

"Welcome Rosemary, nice to see you, I guess I am not in trouble," said Mrs Oluchi on Rosemary's arrival.

"No, my sister Oluchi, I have come to ask for your help and I know you will be able to assist me."

"What kind of help?" Mrs Oluchi asked. "I hope not with money."

"Oluchi, my friend, it is about my daughter Nneka. She will be heading to the city with her uncle, Chief Uzodike, and his wife in about two weeks' time, and honestly I haven't any money and I need some cash to prepare for her departure. Oluchi, I seriously need your help, as I want my Nneka to dress smartly and look as gorgeous as the city girls. I don't want anyone to think of her as just a poor village girl, but as one who has already been in the city. Please, I need your help by asking you to lend me some money, and I pledge to reimburse you as soon as my daughter gets to her uncle in the city and starts making some money."

"So, Rosemary, you mean that I should lend you money and wait until your daughter, Nneka, gets to the city and finds a job, you must be joking," said Oluchi. "What if she gets to the city and can't find a job? What will happen and how will I get my money back from you?"

"Oluchi, if the worst comes to the worst, let me assure you I will not hesitate to sell whatever valuable belongings I have to reimburse you," Rosemary said pointedly.

"Rosemary, you are joking. Please leave my house and go. I have no money to give you, is that clear? Anyway, I advise you to go and ask your other friend, Mrs Ngozi Okoro, to lend you some money. She is very rich and besides, one of her sons, Okeychukwu Aka (Okey boy), is living in the United States of America. He frequently sends US dollars to his mother. I am pretty sure she would be able to offer you any help you request. Please, I would advise you to go and narrate all your stories to Ngozi, OK? I hope she will listen to you even if you pledge to pay her back the money in the next fifty years. She will definitely accept your stories. Now, get out of my house and go please. I have no time to spare with you right now because I am running very late for the market. Today is our Nkwo Umunkwo's open market day and I was supposed to be there at exactly nine o'clock, and what's the time now? It's 11.26 a.m., so please just go, and bye for now."

***

Rosemary went to Mrs Ngozi Okoro to ask for help. On arrival she was met by both Ngozi and her gaunt husband, Chief Nwabueze.

"Madam, what can we do for you and what has brought you to our house so early in the morning?" he enquired.

"Mama Nneka, it is too early to visit us. Did you sleep at all? What can I do for you? I hope everything is fine with you and your family?" Ngozi added.

"Yes Ngozi, we are all fine, thank you," replied Rosemary, full of distrust.

"I have heard from a friend of mine that your daughter, Nneka, is planning to move to the city soon with her uncle, Chief Uzodike. Is it true?"

"Yes, Ngozi, it *is* true and that is the reason why I have come to your house this morning. It would make me happy if you could assist me in any possible way."

Rosemary told Ngozi that she had no money and Chief Uzodike would be coming in two weeks' time to collect Nneka and take her to his house in the city.

"Please, my dear friend, Ngozi, I can assure you that whatever amount you lend me today, honestly as soon as my daughter gets to the city and finds a job, she will be sending it back to me, and I will reimburse you with a huge profit, if you don't mind. I haven't got anyone to ask for help except you."

Ngozi's husband, Chief Nwabueze, interceded by asking his wife to consider Rosemary's plea by trying to help her in any way she could, but his wife had a good memory and did not trust Rosemary.

"By the way, how much money are you hoping to borrow from me?" Ngozi asked.

"Ngozi, I only need a hundred naira."

"So you and your husband cannot afford a hundred naira? Rosemary, are you not ashamed of yourself? Does this mean that you and your shameless and destitute husband, Mr Anaeke, really cannot afford a lousy hundred naira? It's not enough money to purchase all the items your daughter Nneka needs to travel to the city. Rosemary, when will you and your family stop begging?" Ngozi continued, "Enough is enough. Have you forgotten that two years ago you came to my house to ask me for twenty naira and you pledged to return it on an agreed date, but you never came to do so. I kept quiet about it and now you have come back again to ask for more help, while you still owe me twenty naira. Listen, Rosemary, I have made this silly mistake with you before by lending you my money, but this time around I am not going to listen to your sweet-talk again, OK? Last time you swore to me on your family's life and promised to reimburse me my money, but you didn't fulfil your promise. Let me tell you, Rosemary, I don't trust you because I am not even sure if I lent you more money today that you would be able to honour your promise by repaying me. Your sweet mouth is full of lies. Short and painless; please, Mrs Sweet mouth Rosemary, I want you to leave my house and go now."

As Rosemary was leaving Ngozi's house feeling deflated at her friend's rejection, she began to weep through sheer frustration. Ngozi called her back and asked her to provide any valuable belongings, including her family home, as collateral, after which she would reconsider her request. She even went further by requesting that both Rosemary and her husband took an oath again, before she would give her a second chance and lend her the one hundred naira.

Rosemary's husband, Anaeke, wanted nothing to do with such an agreement.

"I am not a party to this agreement, please, my wife Rosemary, think very wisely before you commit yourself. I would prefer to remain perpetually poor rather than borrow money that I cannot afford to repay."

Ngozi, who still doubted that Rosemary would honour their agreement, and wishing to avoid any indignity, tried to make the situation clear to her friend.

"Rosemary, I am willing to offer you help for the sake of Almighty God, by lending you the one hundred naira, but if you fail to repay me on the agreed date, I will not hesitate to confiscate whatever valuables you and your family own, including your dilapidated mud house. Have I made my intentions clear? Rosemary, I would once again advise you to go home, discuss it with your husband and come back by tomorrow, OK?"

***

Soon after Rosemary arrived home, she began to explain to Anaeke all that Ngozi had said. Her husband, who earlier had not endorsed the idea of his wife borrowing money to purchase clothes, shoes and other items for Nneka, was bitterly upset and distressed about what Rosemary had done.

"Rosemary my wife, what if our daughter Nneka fails to send us this money, how will you manage to pay Ngozi back?" Anaeke asked. "You know that Nneka has never been to the city before and I am pretty certain she will be find it hard to adapt to the city lifestyle. She will also find it very difficult to get a good job. What will you do, and how will you get all the money to pay Ngozi back? Bear in mind the fact that you still owe Ngozi the money she lent you some time ago, and now you want to borrow again from the same person a second time. Have you thought about the amount of interest that will accumulate on both loans? Do you really think you and I would be able to afford to reimburse her? Please think wisely before signing any agreement with your friend, Ngozi," he said, trying to make her see that it would be a foolish thing to do.

"Don't say I haven't warned you. Do you honestly want to land yourself in serious trouble that could result in our ugly mud house and whatever meagre valuables we own being repossessed by Ngozi? Rosemary, I am not going to be a party to this agreement, and I have repeatedly warned you to go down another route. You could hire some second-hand clothes including shoes, underwear and the other items that Nneka needs. When she gets to the city with her uncle, she would be able to return all the items to us, then we could return them to the respective owners. This idea is so simple and less cost-effective. All that Nneka would have to do would be to find some empty boxes and send all the items back to us."

Rosemary was quick to reply.

"My husband Anaeke, I don't agree with you and I will be going ahead to approach some other friends of mine for help."

***

As poor Rosemary's search continued, she remembered one friend of hers called Ukamaka, and thought about going to her for assistance this time around.

I will never give up hope and the search for where to borrow the one hundred naira my daughter, Nneka, needs to travel to the city, Rosemary thought. Time is running out. I cannot wait to see Ukamaka.

Rosemary was very determined and quite worried, but her friend Ukamaka was working as a school teacher, therefore, she would be able to offer her help by lending her the money she needed. She knew that the end of the month was fast approaching, so Ukamaka would be receiving her monthly wages. Rosemary decided to go to Ukamaka's house as quickly as possible before she spent her wages.

On arrival at Ukamaka's house, Rosemary was met by a young boy called Udoka, who was standing in front of her friend's house. Rosemary spoke to him.

"Good evening, my son."

"Thank you madam, you are welcome. Madam, may I know who you are and who you are looking for?" Udoka enquired.

"I am Mrs Rosemary Anaeke, the only wife of Anaeke aka Agwuturu Mbe. Young boy, I am here to see Mrs Ukamaka."

"Who is Ukamaka? By the way, madam, don't you know what time it is? It is too late to visit someone at this time of night. Don't you have a watch with you?" asked young Udoka. "Who is Ukamaka?" he repeated. "Where does she live and what does she look like?"

"I was told I might find Ukamaka here."

"Yes I know Ukamaka, she is my mother, but I don't know where she went."

As Rosemary was still talking to the young Udoka, Ukamaka came out of the house and met her on the doorstep.

"Rosemary, I don't need to ask why you have come this evening. I have heard from so many of our friends and neighbours that you have resorted to notorious begging, and so have become one of the unscrupulous fraudsters whom everyone in this neighbourhood knows about. Rosemary, just let me take advantage of this opportunity to advise you as a friend to stop letting yourself down by asking people for money. Please always cut your coat according to your cloth and don't spend more than you earn."

"Ukamaka, you are very much aware of my financial predicament. Right now as I am talking to you my priority is urgently to get together one hundred naira for my daughter Nneka. I need to purchase all the items she requires, and I have asked so many of my friends and neighbours, but no one was willing to offer any help. Even some of my friends, who were motivated and willing to assist me, went on to ask me to provide unthinkable documents and also a guarantor as a form of collateral before they would be able to lend me the sum of one hundred naira. Ukamaka, I know quite well that you are a preceptor, a salary earner. The month has just ended and you will have received your wages, so I was hoping you would be in a position to offer me help."

"Who told you to come and ask me for money, and how do you know that I have received my monthly salary today?" Ukamaka enquired. "If you don't answer my questions I won't be able to help you out."

"No one told me to come to you. Even my husband, Mr Anaeke, did not know who you were, and besides, I was just guessing you might help me."

"Well, I understand," said Ukamaka. "What do you do for a living, Rosemary?"

"I am a local village petty trader," replied Rosemary, unhappy that she had to answer such a question.

"OK, listen to me Rosemary. I really do understand that your present financial predicament is causing you a great deal of concern and distress, as none of your so-called friends and neighbours is willing to help you out. I am pretty sure that if I also refuse to assist you, and you have no other hope of getting the one hundred naira you require, it is highly likely you might maliciously hurt yourself or even become deranged. I have therefore decided on a tough course of action based on the following two conditions. You Rosemary will engage in two days of intensive farm work for me, and after that you will do domestic duties for another three days. These duties will include looking after my children, preparing and cooking food for my family, fetching water from the village public boreholes, keeping my house tidy, washing up and ironing my clothes." Ukamaka continued to explain. "Once all these jobs are successfully completed, eventually you will be able to receive the sum of one hundred naira from me without any reimbursement, but, on the other hand, if you refuse to accept these conditions, I can assure you I will never help you again. This is the way out of your predicament; you can either choose to remain and take up your challenges or you can leave and never return."

In desperation, Rosemary decided to embrace Ukamaka's tough conditions, as she had no other choice.

"Thank you so much for your help, Ukamaka. I will accept the conditions and I am looking forward to the challenges."

***

The following day Rosemary began with her two days of farming work, starting at precisely seven o'clock in the morning and finishing just around six o'clock in the evening. Her work included the cultivation of yams, cassava and maize for the first two days.

Each morning Rosemary left her house in the morning with all her farming tools. She was working for almost eleven hours with neither food nor drinking water. She kept her spirits up by singing her favourite gospel music as she toiled. She had no time for a short break to rest, but kept working continuously until she finished for the day. She worked quite fast to make sure she had completed all her allotted work before leaving. Rosemary worked diligently to please and satisfy Ukamaka in order to avoid any confrontation with her that would make her change her mind or withdraw from helping her further.

Rosemary had completed the first stage of her two days farm work. Next she embarked on harvesting the cassava in the company of her husband, Mr Anaeke. They both started at precisely seven o'clock in the morning with the usual singing and dancing while working with neither food nor drinking water. Rosemary had taken her husband to assist her to complete the work on time, so that she would be able to move on to the final stage of her three days of domestic work in Ukamaka's home the following day.

Unfortunately it was quite worrying when Rosemary and her husband were unable to complete all the work on the second day, therefore, they decided to sleep over in a nearby village at the home of a family friend of her husband, Mr Ikenna. He lived very close to where she and her husband were working. They wanted to wake up very early the following morning to finish the work before Ukamaka arrived for the final inspection.

From the beginning, Ukamaka had repeatedly warned Rosemary that she expected her to complete her two days farm work within the set two days and take no longer, so that Rosemary could immediately start on the domestic and child minding duties Ukamaka had planned. Rosemary was afraid Ukamaka would turn up the following morning and find the farm work unfinished.

***

The next day Rosemary embarked on her final three days of domestic work in Ukamaka's house. On her arrival she was met by Ukamaka and her two children, Ogbonna and Nwabueze. Ukamaka took Rosemary around the house and showed her where the lavatory, bathroom and kitchen were.

"Rosemary, you are very welcome in my house, and I want you to relax and feel at home. Look after yourself and take care of my two boys, OK? Please look after my children very well; they are well mannered and obedient," Ukamaka said. "The reason why I am giving you these instructions is that I am going away for the next two or three days, OK?" She asked Rosemary again, "Do you understand your work description?"

"Yes, madam," Rosemary replied.

One hour after Ukamaka's departure, Rosemary began her domestic work by cooking food for the evening meal for the two boys left in her care. Soon after, she took the two boys to the bathroom for a shower. After giving the boys a shower, Rosemary served them their dinner. Twenty-five minutes later, the boys finished their dinner and Rosemary sent them to their respective bedrooms.

Rosemary returned to the kitchen to resume her chores, washing up the plates and cleaning up any mess she had made. She also tidied up all the other rooms. Soon after, she took a short break to have her own evening meal and to watch television for precisely half an hour, then she made sure that Ukamaka's two boys had settled down for the night. Next, she quickly fetched the water from the nearby public boreholes. She had to go more than five times until the empty plastic containers were full of water for the next day. After that she went to bed.

***

Rosemary slept for only four hours, as she had to get up very early in the morning in order to have enough time to get breakfast ready before the boys awoke. She vacuumed all the rooms, including the living room and the children's room. She swept the kitchen and mopped the bathroom.

Soon after, she woke up the boys and took them one after the other to the bathroom to get them ready for school. Rosemary gave them the breakfast she had prepared before dropping the boys off at school.

On returning to Ukamaka's house Rosemary continue her chores. She began with hand washing Ukamaka's clothes and those of her friend's children as quickly as possible. Next she did the ironing for another two hours. Throughout the two days in her job in Ukamaka's house she was working non-stop. She was so occupied with the domestic work that she spent much of her time in the kitchen doing her chores.

Rosemary had to get the children's afternoon tea ready before picking them up from school. After cooking both meals, Rosemary hurried to the rural school to collect Ukamaka's boys and take them home. She made sure that they were well fed and well looked after. She helped Ukamaka's children to do their school homework then once again went to fetch water from the public boreholes located just half a mile away. She had no bicycle or a wheelbarrow; however, she went back and forth fetching the water at least four times a day.

***

Thank God she is back, thought Rosemary.

Ukamaka arrived home after her two-day trip to Kafachan.

"Ukamaka, my one and only friend, how was your trip?" Rosemary enquired.

"It was brilliant." Ukamaka went on to thank Rosemary for looking after her two boys. "Have this one hundred naira from me Rosemary, and you are free to go. You have successfully completed your farm work and your domestic job, and I am so grateful. Once again thank you so much for your help. I am really sorry about the inconvenience, but I just wish you and your family all the best for the future, OK? Bye and have a nice evening."

"And you too, thank you *so* much. It is very much appreciated indeed, God bless," said Rosemary.

When a delighted and irrepressible Rosemary was making her way back home half an hour later, she lifted her hands up to heaven; she was singing and dancing on the road. She sniffed the one hundred naira twice and said:

"One hundred naira so this is you, I have finally got you. God, you are so kind and wonderful."

***

When Rosemary arrived home she shouted out very loudly, so that anyone speaking could not be heard.

"Come here quick, Nneka, my daughter, and where is your father?"

"He just went out" Nneka replied, quickly embracing her mum after the initial shock of seeing her. "Welcome home, Mum."

"Thanks, my lovely daughter, and how are you?"

"Fine Mum."

"Can you see this envelope in my hand?" asked Rosemary.

"Yes Mum, I can see it," said Nneka.

Rosemary asked Nneka if she could guess what the contents of the envelope might be. Nneka had a very strong feeling that the contents might possibly be cash.

"Mum, is it money inside the envelope?"

"Yes, it is money," said Rosemary. Rosemary went on to tease her daughter by asking her to touch the envelope. "Touch it and don't be afraid, this is the sum of one hundred naira we have been looking for all along. I have finally got it at after a disastrous five days of contemporary servitude at the hands of my parsimonious and stubborn so-called friend, Ukamaka. It was never to be forgotten experience, but I give thanks to God Almighty, who made it possible for us to obtain this money through Ukamaka. God has just heard our prayers and cries."

"Mum, I don't even know where to begin to thank you. I don't even think words can explain how much I appreciate all you have suffered for me. You have been a wonderful mum and I am very proud of you, and very pleased that it's all over now. Mum, thank you once again. I greatly appreciate your generosity. You are such an amazing and tremendous mum and I hope in the near future I will be able to repay you in any way possible."

"You are highly acclaimed. Thank you too, my daughter Nneka," said Rosemary.

While Rosemary and Nneka were dancing and rejoicing, Mr Anaeke arrived home and quickly spoke to his wife and daughter.

"What is all this dancing and shouting about?"

"My husband, I have made it."

"What did you make?" asked Mr Anaeke.

"I have got the money from Ukamaka," replied Rosemary.

"What a surprise! Can we go out for Nneka's shopping now?"

"Yes, of course, dress up and let's go shopping," said Rosemary.

She asked Nneka if she was eager to go to the market with them.

"Yes Mum," she replied, "but have you both forgotten it is market day and my uncle, Chief Uzodike, said he would be coming to our house to pick me up?"

"*Ewoo. Chimoo*, I am lost!" her dad exclaimed "She is a hundred per cent correct; I had forgotten about it. OK, it is never too late, let's go shopping. Get ready quickly, and let's go before Chief Uzodike and his wife arrive. Rosemary, please don't forget I need a pair of trousers."

"My husband, you don't need any trousers, you have got enough pairs. You need trousers for what?"

"Rosemary, are you asking me what I need trousers for? Have you forgotten that I only have one pair of shorts, not even a pair of trousers? Let me ask you, do you want me to wear these ugly dirty shorts when we are expecting an important visitor? Not only women can dress and look gorgeous, men need to do it as well."

He went on threatening his wife. If she was not willing to purchase him just one pair of trousers, he informed her, he would not be going to the market.

"Fair enough then stay behind, but I am going with Nneka. Anaeke, you are nothing but a braggart. You have been boasting all along and you cannot even afford to buy yourself just one pair of trousers, and you just called yourself a man. Are you not ashamed of yourself? You were here when I left for five days to struggle to get this money together, and you call yourself a family man. You cannot even afford one hundred naira to buy your daughter Nneka's items she needs to travel to the city with her uncle. Anaeke, now it is your turn to go and beg to borrow money to buy yourself a pair of trousers, foolish man. You know quite well how hard it was for me to get this money, and I will not concern myself about anything other than spending it on Nneka."

"If you are not going to buy what you promised me, fair enough, but when your brother, Chief Uzodike, and his wife, Oluchi, arrive to pick up our daughter I am definitely not going to be around. I don't want to let myself down by wearing old clothes that I should not be wearing."

"Anaeke, cut your cloth according to your size," said Rosemary. "What about the tracksuit I purchased for you two months ago? Why not wear that when my brother and his wife arrive? You want to dress like a millionaire, but you cannot even afford one common naira."

"The tracksuit you bought for me is no longer here; I gave it to my friend, Okeke."

"When did you give Okeke your tracksuit? I hope you did not sell it to him."

"Yes, I sold it to Okeke for five naira last month when I needed money to buy a pair of shoes to travel along with my friends for Chief Onwu's daughter's wedding," said Anaeke.

"Since when have you started selling clothes? I hope in the near future you will not sell anything from this house No wonder I saw you wearing a pair of beautiful black shoes some time ago. My mind was telling me to ask you where you got the money to buy such an expensive pair of shoes, but I forgot and it went out of my mind completely."

"Rosemary, don't forget that conditions make the crayfish bend. Actually, I did not intend to sell my tracksuit to Okeke, but I did so because I needed those shoes very urgently. I can no longer afford to buy myself anything. I did not want to bother you by asking you to buy the shoes, as I knew you had a lot of responsibilities and burdens facing you at the time."

"But Anaeke, you should have asked me before selling your tracksuit to Mr Okeke. What if I had seen him in the street wearing your tracksuit? I would have embarrassed him by asking how he came by the tracksuit, without knowing that you had sold it to him. How would you be reacting if you had not been told?"

"OK, I do apologise for not letting you know about selling my tracksuit," said Anaeke. He assured Rosemary that he would never engage in such an act of debasement again. "If you still cannot afford to purchase me a pair of trousers, I will look for an alternative. I will change my mind about staying here and wear my blue cardigan, which I had reserved for Christmas, if you wouldn't mind. Your brother, Chief Uzodike, is just an in-law to me, not even a brother, so I don't see any reason why I should feel ashamed. It is you, my wife Rosemary, who will feel the shame, not me, because Chief Uzodike is your brother."

Anaeke reminded his wife what had happened previously in their neighbourhood, when one of their family friends, Mr Okuku's daughter, was making preparations to travel to the city to be reunited with her husband.

"What actually happened that very day when Okuku's son in-law came to pick up Okuku's daughter, Vanessa, and take her to the city?" asked Anaeke.

"My husband, I cannot remember and besides, it was a long time ago," said Rosemary.

"So, you cannot remember now, so even you cannot recollect some things. OK Rosemary, have you forgotten that both Okuku and his wife were dressed in beautiful white lace, looking as glamorous as a celebrity couple."

"OK, I remember now" said Rosemary, adding, "my husband Anaeke, have you also forgotten that Okuku's son in-law, Nwabueze, was the one who bought that white lace for Okuku and his wife? The lace was made in the city and not in the village. Okuku's son in-law lives in the city where he purchased it. Let me ask you one simple question; have you got any close relatives of yours living in the city? If you have, why not tell them to send us similar costumes, so we can look as well dressed and posh as Okuku and his wife? I want you to understand that Okuku's daughter's situation was different from Nneka's. Vanessa was going to the city that time to be reunited with her husband, while our daughter is moving to the city with her uncle, Chief Uzodike, as a common housemaid. Can you see the difference now?"

"Yes, it is well understood," said Anaeke.

Later on Rosemary apologised to her husband for her anger, and assured him she would get the pair of trousers he requested. She told him to stop moaning and calm down, then gave him a warning.

"If you continue to harass me, I am not going to buy the trousers, so let's bury the hatchet and quickly get ready to go to the market, as we are running out of time. Anaeke, put on your clothes and we will get on our way, OK?"

"Give me two minutes and I will get prepared as quickly as possible," Anaeke replied.

***

Half an hour later, Anaeke and Rosemary arrived at the market. They started arguing again after Anaeke spotted a boutique that specialised in elite and fashionable items such as clothing and jewellery. He quickly entered the boutique and saw the current season's patterned palazzo trousers. Feeling very clever, he hurriedly asked his wife to purchase the trousers for him.

"These are exactly the type of trousers I am looking for, so please can you buy them for me now before we start on Nneka's shopping?"

"Anaeke my husband, why can't you just be patient and wait until we have finished Nneka's shopping, then we can go ahead and buy all the other things you require as I promised earlier. Have you forgotten what I told you before we left the house? Calm down and relax, and you will eventually get your trousers today. The patient dog eats the fattest bone."

"No, I cannot wait any longer because these are the exact size and colour that will go with my white short-sleeved shirt, which I am looking forward to wearing when Chief Uzodike and his wife arrive. If you don't get them now before we start Nneka's shopping, we may not have enough money left over to pick them up, or someone else might buy them."

"No one is going to buy these trousers and I assure you this pair will remain here until we come back with the payment.

"I am afraid they might be gone when we come back to pay for the trousers. If you are serious about buying them for me, and since you cannot make the full payment, why not make a part payment to the boutique owner, to assure me that the trousers will remain intact until we return to make the full payment?"

"Let me go and have a word with the boutique owner to ask her to reserve the trousers for us, so we can collect them within the next two to three hours," suggested Rosemary.

Husband and wife met the shop owner and explained what they intended to do. The boutique owner quickly said she would reserve the trousers for Anaeke for another two hours until they returned with the full payment.

"Are you happy now?" Rosemary asked.

"I will be happy when you buy what you promised me."

"You are so funny! Could you repeat what you have just said?"

"I said I am going to be happy when you keep your promise. Do you understand me?"

"Yes I do," said Rosemary, then she burst into laughter. "Why do we sometimes behave like kids? Please stop it and refrain from this selfish attitude of yours."

They returned home not having purchased one item for Nneka.

***

A few days later, with preparations for Nneka's departure underway, Rosemary and Anaeke went to purchase the following items for their daughter: two pairs of slippers; one skirt and blouse; two pairs of earrings; one make-up kit; one dressing gown and four pairs of underwear. After buying everything their daughter required for her new life with her uncle to the city, they immediately went to collect Anaeke's trousers from the boutique. However, Rosemary and her husband were met by the boutique owner, Jessica, who earnestly enquired how she could help them.

"Jessica, we have come to pick up my husband's trousers, which we asked you to put on hold for us two days ago."

"Sorry, it was not this boutique, and besides we don't keep items on hold for our customers, maybe you and your husband are in the wrong boutique," said Jessica.

"So Jessica, are you saying that you do not recognise me and my husband form when we came with the deposit for one pair of navy blue trousers just a few days ago?" asked Rosemary. "Are you saying that you did not receive any form of payment as a deposit from us? If this is the case, Jessica, you must be a thief."

"Have you ever caught me stealing before?" asked Jessica.

"I don't know. A thief does not have any noticeable marks on their face," Rosemary replied.

"I blame myself for wasting my time talking to a dirty arrogant woman like you," said Jessica.

The boutique owner denied accepting any money as a deposit and pretended not to know Rosemary and her husband, Anaeke. She demanded that they should leave her boutique immediately, and failure to do so would result in both being chased by the angry market mob. Rosemary and her husband refused to leave the boutique. Anaeke, who had kept silent, was bitterly upset by Jessica's attitude, then spoke to her angrily.

"You must be joking, Jessica, you are nothing but a light-fingered and shameless woman. Are you not the one who collected our money two days ago and asked us to return in the next few hours to pick up my trousers? Don't forget that I know your husband, Mr Gregory, quite well and, if refuse to return my deposit, I can assure you that I will report this matter to him and I am pretty sure he will be bitterly upset with you."

Jessica repeatedly asked Rosemary and her husband to leave her store

"This is my last warning to both of you to leave my boutique. I am going to say once again that I want both of you to leave, but whether you agree with me or not, you are a stupid and discourteous couple. You must go now before I count to twenty."

"Who are you calling stupid and discourteous?" asked Rosemary. "You are nothing but a coward. If you don't refrain from these fraudulent acts of yours, you will inevitably find yourself in a very hostile situation. We are not afraid of you and we are not going to move from your boutique until we get our deposit back."

"OK, wait and see. Let me see who will be running when it happens" said Jessica.

All of a sudden a fight broke out between the two women. Rosemary grabbed and squeezed one of Jessica's breasts as she lay on the floor crying and shouting loudly for help, but unfortunately no one came to her rescue. Anaeke was busy watching and directing his wife on the best strategy and tactics to use in order to beat Jessica mercilessly, so that she would never be involved in any fraudulent activities with anyone she came into contact with in the future. Whilst being punched and beaten by Rosemary, Jessica was shouting:

"*Ole, ole* (thief, thief)! I need help, please someone come to my rescue, I am being attacked by two armed robbers in my boutique. Please, I need help urgently before they kill me."

Anaeke was still very busy, coaching and advising Rosemary on how to apply the best tactics to defeat Jessica.

"Please make sure you teach her a lesson, OK? Use any harmful and unreasonable tactics on her, OK? If you wish you can destroy her two eyes so that she will never see again. Start with punching, but don't use karate; I can see she is good at that, and given the slightest opportunity she will throw you to the floor. Don't go too close to her, OK? Use your head to punch her face, OK?"

A few minutes later, Jessica was still crying loudly and yelling for help. She was ignored by the few individuals who were standing and laughing instead of separating the two women. They were all cheering, encouraging and supporting Rosemary to teach Jessica a lesson. She continued to shout very loudly:

"*Ole, ole!*"

Jessica was pretending she was under attack by the armed robbers, but luckily for her a

passer-by heard her shouting, crying and calling for assistance, and instantly recognised her.

"Oh, my God, she is my customer, Jessica. I know her quite well. What did she do?" Grace

enquired. "Who are these two people attacking her? I hope they are not armed robbers. How can a poor innocent woman be attacked in broad daylight by armed robbers?" Grace shouted loudly and shook her head. "God forbid, I am going immediately to inform both the angry mob and the market vigilantes, so that they will come to her rescue before she is shot by these armed robbers."

Grace ran off quickly to alert the vigilantes, her two hands on her head as she cried out:

"Look at that poor woman, Jessica, being beaten and robbed by armed robbers for no reason. They are attacking Jessica, they must never go free and they must be apprehended by the vigilantes. Let's wait and see."

A short while later, Grace and a large angry mob were coming with their machetes. Some were carrying gallons of petrol, others were carrying tyres. As soon as Rosemary and Anaeke saw them approaching, they hurriedly left Jessica to run away from the vicinity. They were quite well aware that once they were apprehended by the mob, one of them would definitely be stoned to death or set alight. They were chased by the angry mob that were shouting angrily with raised machetes, tyres and gallons of petrol, intent upon either killing or burning one of them alive. They thought Rosemary and Anaeke were potential armed robbers, as they had been informed by Grace that Jessica was under attack by two thieves.

Luckily for Rosemary and her husband, they were rescued by a taxi driver, who saw them trying to escape from the angry mob.

"Why are you two running?" he enquired.

"My brother, we are being chased by this angry mob you see coming," said Anaeke.

"And what did you and your wife do?" asked the taxi driver.

"Sorry taxi driver, it's a really long story and I cannot explain it to you right now. However, I will be able to tell you the bone of contention when the situation has calmed down, OK? Please bear with us."

"Yes, I understand and I can see both of you are under intense pressure, therefore, get into the car and let's move quickly before we are besieged by this angry rabble," said the taxi driver.

As soon as Rosemary and her husband got into the car, he quickly drove off and immediately dropped them off in a safe place.

***

Later Rosemary was miserable, and blamed Anaeke for being so obstinate about extraneous things.

"Anaeke, have you seen what you have caused us now? We have lost our entire deposit money paid to that crook, Jessica, and also would have nearly been tortured and beaten to death or burned alive by the angry mob, but God was so kind. We are so lucky to be alive with the help of the taxi driver who came to our rescue. What would have happened if we had been caught by those dangerous individuals? Please, my husband Anaeke, I don't want to die early because of you, so let it be the first and last such incident that occurs. I will no longer tolerate it and do not expect it to ever happen again, OK?"

Rosemary continued to rebuke her husband.

"In fact, I honestly don't know how this shanty town of ours and our enemies would have reacted if we had been caught by that dangerous mob. I think it would have been a kind of mixed reaction between two factions, resulting in one group showing a kind of concern by trying to sympathise with us, while our enemies indicated less concern and mistrust by trying to ridicule us. You should have known better by using your common sense and behaving like a responsible adult instead of focusing on irrelevant matters like trousers, because you want to dress and look posh when Chief Uzodike and his wife arrive. I also want to look fashionable when they arrive. This is all I have been hearing from you, an adult, almost every hour of every day in this house. You call yourself a responsible household husband? It is a shame. Anaeke, instead of helping me out to get the vital items ready for our daughter, you were so anxious to obtain cash to buy trousers to look stylish for Chief Uzodike and his wife's arrival. Since we have lost our little cash to that crook Jessica, which we would have used to buy your trousers, and have no hope of getting more cash, what do you think you can do now to get more money to buy yourself a pair of trousers?"

"Relax your mind Rosemary and don't panic; there must be a solution to this problem. I will be looking for an alternative now, OK?" replied Anaeke.

"What alternative do you in mind, Anaeke?" asked Rosemary.

"I am considering going to ask a friend of mine, Mr Udoka, if he can offer me help by swapping my bicycle for one of his agbadas."

"I think that's a good idea," replied Rosemary, adding, "just go quickly and have a word with him, since you know he is in a position to offer you help as a close friend."

***

Anaeke arrived at his friend's house and was met by Mr Udoka's wife, Eunice, who spoke to him briskly.

"Mr Anaeke, my husband's friend, what has brought you to our house? So, you just remember my husband today after a long period of four years. Anyway, how is your immediate family? I hope they are all in good spirits. Come inside the room, have a seat and let me go and look for Udoka."

Half an hour later, Udoka entered the living room, they embraced each other and shouted joyously.

"Anaeke, my dear friend, it's a long time since we met, where have you been? I have been searching for you. How is your business?" asked Udoka.

"My business just collapsed, so I have nothing tangible to do at the moment. We are really struggling to make ends meet," replied Anaeke.

"That is enough, Anaeke, I have heard enough, OK?" said Udoka. "How may I help you, my one and only friend, Anaeke?"

"I have come to ask you for a favour," said Anaeke.

"What favour?"

"I actually came to ask you if it is possible that you can help me out with one of your agbadas."

"What do you mean by helping you out with my agbada? Anaeke, please explain what you mean. I do not understand how my agbada can help you." said Udoka, puzzled.

"OK, let me try to explain to you very concisely. I am asking if you can help me by swapping my bicycle for one of your agbadas."

"What do you want with my agbada? Don't you know that all my agbadas are very expensive and, therefore, for wealthy men like myself and not poor people like you, Anaeke?"

"Oh, sorry my friend Udoka, I actually forgot to mention to you earlier that my daughter Nneka is soon moving to the city with her uncle, Chief Uzodike. We are expecting Chief Uzodike's arrival at any moment now, which is why I have come to ask you if it is possible for you to lend me one of your agbadas, and I promise to return it to you as soon as I am through with my in-law Chief Uzodike's visit to my house," said Anaeke.

"Udoka, you must realise how uneasy I am at the moment for a rich man like my in-law, Chief Uzodike, to visit a poor man like me for the first time. I really don't know which way to turn and I don't even know the kind of food and drinks Chief Uzodike and his wife Oluchi will be requesting. I do believe if you were the person Chief Uzodike and his wife were visiting for the first time, and I know quite well you must be very confident having been in similar situations before, you would definitely find it much easier than me, who has never been a rich man."

"Anaeke, what do you mean by me being in such a situation before?" asked Udoka.

"Have you forgotten that you were once among the five richest men in this village of Umuobom with so many properties, cars and a chain of companies? Where has all your money and wealth gone now?"

"Anaeke, let me ask you, are you coming to my own house to insult me? Listen and let me warn you now, if you don't shut up I will ask you to leave my house immediately. I thought by now you would have left behind this egoistic and arrogant behaviour of yours."

"Udoka, I did not say any nasty word by cursing, swearing and blaspheming you, and besides, I was only trying to remind you about the past, OK? Please don't be offended. I want you to understand this in our common Igbo proverb which says, 'One who first enters bush knows more about that particular bush than one who has never entered before'."

"Please, I don't understand your proverb. I am trying to calm you down and you still have the audacity to insult me all over again in my own house," said Udoka.

"Udoka, I am not insulting you. I can explain the meaning of the proverb to you. It means that the dowry your father paid to your mother's parents during her marriage was a complete waste," said Anaeke.

"Anaeke, did someone tell you to come to my house to slander me? Please, I want to know. Do you understand that is why I refuse to associate myself so closely with destitute and poor church rats like you?"

"By the way Udoka, who are you calling a destitute and poor church rat? Is it because I have come to you for help?" asked Anaeke.

"I have heard enough from you today. I think you should make your way back to your house now, OK? I don't want to see you here again. I want you to go on your way before I start counting up to ten, or I will call one of my dangerous dogs to chase you out of my house. As you are leaving my wife will throw one of my agbadas through the window for you, and never bother to return it to me. I honestly don't want to see you again in my house, foolish man," said Udoka.

Udoka asked his so-called friend what his agbada had to do with Anaeke's in-law coming to his house to pick up his daughter. Anaeke told him he just wanted to wear it in order to look very smart and posh.

"What about your wife, Rosemary, Anaeke? Is she also going to dress up and look posh when her brother, Chief Uzodike, or whatever you called him, arrives at your house?"

"I don't really know," replied Anaeke.

"Why don't you know? She is your wife isn't she? Rosemary is the person who is expected to look smart when Chief Uzodike and his wife turn up at your house, because he is her elder brother and not an insolvent and desperate man like you. Anaeke, why have you been worrying about where to borrow an agbada when you are not even related to Chief Uzodike? I think you must be a braggart. You are a nonentity who cannot even afford to buy just the cheapest agbada for yourself, and you come to my house and insult me. No one has ever insulted me before in my own house. Please go and collect one of my agbadas through the window from my wife, so that you will look posh when Chief Uzodike and his wife arrive, what a stupid man you are. Please go quickly now, as I want to close my door, OK?"

"Thank you so much for your help," said Anaeke.

"Hey, hey, please Anaeke, I don't want any appreciation from an ungrateful coward like you, I just want you to leave my house as quickly as possible," said Udoka.

"Bye Mr Udoka."

"Bye yourself Anaeke."

***

Anaeke returned home following his attempt to swap his bicycle for Udoka's agbada. Shortly afterwards Nneka's uncle, Chief Uzodike, and his wife Oluchi arrived to pick up Nneka to travel along with them to the city.

As Chief Uzodike and his wife were seated in the living room talking to Rosemary and Nneka, Anaeke became very emotional and hurriedly sent Peter, one of his close friends, to invite the elders and some of his neighbours to come and welcome his in-law, Chief Uzodike, and his wife, as Nneka's sending-off party was about to begin. Anaeke then went to try to put on his agbada.

Everone gathered at Anaeka's compound. Anaeke briskly stood up as a mark of courtesy to the elders, as it was required in Igbo land to greet both the elders and senior citizens.

"My elders, I am greeting you all. We are here today to witness my daughter's sending-off party, and most importantly to meet my one and only in-law, Chief Uzodike, and his gorgeous wife Oluchi, who came all the way from the beautiful city of Lagos to be with us today. You are all welcome. I would like to ask the elders and those of you who are present here today to help me to thank my in-law and his wife for coming to take away some responsibility from me by looking after my daughter Nneka."

Soon after Anaeke's welcome speech, the traditional ruler of the host village, Eze Agu, who was the head of the elders, spoke briefly.

"We thank you both, Chief Uzodike and your beautiful wife Oluchi, for coming to release Anaeke's burden, as we all aware that the more you care, the better your child does. Our elders always say going to the city is never the case, but returning is always the case. On behalf of the community and Anaeke's family, I ask Chief Uzodike to take good care of our sister Nneka, by making sure she is well looked after, and most importantly by trying to assist her to fulfil her professional aspiration and to achieve her true potential. She intends to become a teacher. As you all know, education is the greatest form of social change. I would like to make it absolutely clear to Chief Uzodike and his wife that we need action in this town, not empty promises. Thank you both for coming."

Shortly after the traditional ruler's speech, Chief Uzodike thanked Anaeke and his elders for their impeccable hospitality, and he promised to do whatever it took to assist Nneka in any way possible.

"I am going to help Nneka by making her dreams a reality. In an attempt to achieve great erudition and to eradicate illiteracy, I am going to ensure that Nneka furthers her education by continuing from where she stopped due to her parents' substantial financial predicament. It is very important that I will also pay her educational expenses and ensure that she enrols in one of the highly reputable and elite colleges in the city, and hopefully as a result she will be able to realise something tangible by achieving her academic targets and future ambitions."

Chief Uzodike further pledged to treat Nneka as his own daughter. He explained that everyone in his household was treated equally and there was never any favouritism or preferential treatment.

"What I did for my own children, I am going to do for Nneka," said Chief Uzodike.

He insisted that corporal punishment such as smacking and caning was inevitable and inescapable in his household and, as a result, whoever was found to be impertinent would be punished as a zero tolerance policy and also an initiative to crack down on impropriety in his household.

"There is a saying that my child is yours and yours is mine. No one should be left alone to suffer or be ignored, but rather everyone should be treated equally with respect and dignity."

The welcoming speech demanded that Nneka should be permitted to go home to see her parents quite often; however, Chief Uzodike pledged to give Nneka the opportunity to visit her parents in the village only biannually. Chief Uzodike promised financial incentives for both Nneka and her parents. He eventually concluded his speech by assuring both the elders of the host community and Nneka's parents that he owed a duty of care and protection to everyone in his household, including Nneka. He asked Anaeke and Rosemary if they had any objections regarding what he had pledged for Nneka.

"Have you and your wife got any questions about or anything to add to what I have just said?" asked Chief Uzodike.

"Yes, firstly Chief Uzodike, thank you for taking the time to come here, and I would once again thank you both for coming to our rescue precisely when our daughter Nneka so needs your assistance." Anaeke went on to add a few words in relation to what Chief Uzodike had just pronounced. "Education is my top priority for Nneka. As I can no longer afford to send her to further her education due to my financial predicament and being economically inactive in my family, I am glad that you are here to help us by assuring me that my daughter Nneka will be attending school as soon as she gets to the city with you. Imagine such a young girl like my Nneka having no basic education, so how would she cope in the future when she is ready to get married to a man of her choice? Many men in this present day are eager to marry a clumsy inept girl, which in my perspective is absolutely inexorable."

Anaeke also indicated that any act of brutality or callousness towards his daughter would not be tolerated or endured patiently by his wife Rosemary and himself. He pleaded with Chief Uzodike and Oluchi to avoid causing any kind of problems for Nneka, and reminded them to look after her well and endeavour to ensure that she was not going to be kept in the house as a slave.

Soon after Anaeke's speech to persuade Chief Uzodike and his wife to show pity on his daughter, everyone quickly hugged each other.

"Thank you so much, my brother, for your wonderful initiative and the great opportunity you are giving our daughter Nneka by taking her along with you to dwell in the city," said Rosemary. "We here in her village know quite well that there are better prospects in the city than in the village. Everyone is delighted that Nneka is going with you both today and hopefully in the near future, if everything goes according to plan, she will be able to rescue other families who are in a similar situation."

Anaeke spoke to his daughter.

"I wish you the very best of luck, OK?"

"Mum and Dad, it is time to go now. Please, I want you both to look after each other well," said Nneka.

"Stay well with your uncle and his family, and please don't forget to keep in touch with us. Have a safe trip to the beautiful city of Lagos, and we will be looking forward to hearing from you soon," said Anaeke.

Chief Uzodike, Oluchi and Nneka got into the car when the chauffeur arrived. They shut the car doors quickly and immediately drove off with Nneka smiling and waving to her parents and some of her close relatives who had come to witness her departure.

Two

Nneka went to the city with her uncle, Chief Uzodike, full of confidence that she would be going back to school to continue her education as quickly as possible as her uncle had promised. At the time she had no idea that her uncle would not keep his word. Nneka soon realised that he did not intend to send her back to school, and was not willing to fulfil the promises he made to her parents. She became quite apprehensive and very worried, suspecting that something might have gone wrong, so she tried to reach out to her uncle and his wife, which was a waste of time.

Three months later, Nneka intended to return to her parent's home in the village at the earliest possible opportunity before the situation turned ugly. Since her arrival she had always been busy with the domestic jobs in her uncle's house. She had not spoken to her uncle, due to the fact that she was occupied with her domestic duties for twenty-four hours a day. She anxiously waited and expected to hear from her uncle.

One evening at about eight thirty when Chief Uzodike arrived home from his office duties Nneka was becoming frustrated and incensed with him as none of the promises he had made had been met. She hurriedly went to her uncle to speak to him.

"Uncle, when do you think I will go back to school to resume my studies? I am running out of patience now. How long will I have to wait? Don't forget that you promised my parents that you were going to make sure I went back to school to continue my education as soon as I got to the city."

"Let me ask you, Nneka, when did you arrive in the city? I am looking forward to enrolling you in one of the most reputable and elite colleges in the city, and when I have been able to find one I am going to let you know. I am so sorry for the delay and would like to reassure you that I am doing everything I can to ensure you get back to college to continue your education as soon as possible. I understand your concerns, but please calm down and relax. I don't really understand why you teenagers don't exercise some patience these days. There is no cause for alarm. I told you that you will continue your education, it is only a question of time, OK?"

"It is not really necessary that you enrol me in one of the most reputable and expensive colleges here in the city, as what my situation requires now is to get back and further my education. Any kind of college will do whether reputable or non-reputable. Uncle, if you are unwilling to send me back to school please let me know as there are some other interesting possibilities for me. You might as well send me back to my parents. I am willing and ready to go home if you cannot fulfil your promise."

"Stop moaning, Nneka, you know quite well my top priority is to ensure that you further your education and, as I told you earlier, I am going to fulfil all my promises made to you, sooner rather than later," her uncle replied.

"Nneka, please be quiet and stop moaning," said Oluchi. "Let me ask you, do you know how difficult it is to find a reputable college here in the city of Lagos? I know quite well how worried my husband has been about finding you a place in one of the most highly reputable and conveniently located colleges in the city. You know nothing about this city and besides, you are nothing but a novice, therefore, you should shut your dirty stinking mouth and get back into the kitchen to continue your domestic chores. Nneka, I am saying enough is enough, and let me remind you once again that you should not forget that you were hired for just two reasons; firstly to look after my children and secondly to assist with the domestic chores," continued Oluchi. "It is up to my husband and I to decide your future; however, it is not going to be under duress. We are only trying to help you and your destitute parents who cannot even afford to send you and your siblings to school. We were only trying to help out so that you will be able to achieve something tangible that could help you in the future."

Nneka's extreme unhappiness and distress brought her uncle's home into disarray after his wife's outrageous and disgusting remarks towards her, after which she began to cry.

"Please Aunt Oluchi I really want to know what has gone wrong? What did I actually do to you that justifies the insults you have aimed at me and my poor parents, who are in the village struggling to make ends meet? If you truly feel that I have wronged you in any way, fair enough, you can go ahead and do whatever you like to me, but not to my parents, OK? They do not deserve to be insulted and joked about, and you should understand that an insult to my parents is likewise an insult to me. Madam Jezebel Aunt Oluchi, please stop insulting my parents, I am warning you for the second time now. If you continue like this I am going to make a serious complaint against you to your husband, Chief Uzodike. Since I came into my uncle's home I have been made to work twenty-four hours a day taking care of everyone in this household, including washing your dirty clothes, but still you are not satisfied. If you don't want me to stay in this house any more just tell me so that I can arrange for my parents to come and pick me up."

Nneka had complained to her uncle before about his wife's inconsistent, sceptical and unpredictable attitude. She now reacted angrily in response to Oluchi's criticism of herself and her parents and she went on to challenge Oluchi by calling her a callous, discourteous, dastardly, fat ugly bitch.

I am not going to allow Aunt Oluchi to try to terrorise and threaten me anymore, Nneka thought, especially when I have never been unwilling to listen to her extraneous advice, however, I will not be afraid of her. If she fails to respect me then I am not going to respect her - respect is always a reciprocal. I am deeply upset and disappointed, because what I am going through now wasn't what I expected from my own uncle. Chief Uzodike and his wife are cunning and can no longer be trusted. What shall I do? I have never seen such obstreperous and mutinous behaviour in my life. I am running out of time, in fact I am going to do whatever it takes in order to escape this confinement of mine before it gets too late for me.

Nneka knew quite well that it was not going to be easy to escape from my uncle's house. She saw herself as a prisoner behind bars, but she remained confident and hopeful that she would return to my parent's home as soon as possible. She blamed herself for wanting to be in a different location with someone she trusted in order to have better prospects, but without knowing he had skeletons in the cupboard. She was so depressed, stressed out, lonely and bored because her uncle and his wife had ruined her life. She felt betrayed in every way.

Nneka was not allowed out of the house, and was also not permitted to have a mobile phone. She knew quite well that any attempt to escape from her uncle's home was foolhardy, but she was infuriated and felt humiliated and insulted by her Aunt Oluchi's persistent verbal abuse.

***

Nneka was thinking how to return to her parents in the village while she was busy in the kitchen cooking an evening meal. Oluchi surprised her by coming into the kitchen to demand an explanation from her. She asked Nneka who gave her the power and impetus to interrupt her when she was talking to her.

"How dare you Nneka, and who are you by the way?"

Nneka began to explain to her, but she was not given the opportunity to express and defend herself, as she was expeditiously slapped and punched continuously until she fell down onto the floor.

"This is just the beginning and more punishments are on the way. If you are going to remain in this house you must learn how to behave and you must always adhere to my rules, or one day you will see hot boiling water poured over your dirty body."

Nneka was crying very loudly due to the gravity of the serious injuries she had sustained at the hands of her aunt. She managed to speak through her sobs.

"Yes, I can understand now the reason why my father was initially opposed to the whole idea of me coming to the city with you both, but eventually he changed his mind and agreed with my mother to allow me to travel here. In hindsight, if I had known about this, I would have made no attempt to travel to the city. I didn't leave my parent's home in the village to come to the beautiful city of Lagos to be tormented by my own uncle's wicked and vicious wife."

"Listen Nneka, don't get upset, I assure you that you are not going to be maltreated and killed in this house. My husband and I did not bring you here to work like a slave, but to assist you to enrol at the top city college to enable you to learn how to read and write so you can achieve your potential in the near future."

"Aunt, please don't try to pull the wool over my eyes. I know what I am saying is true. Coming from a poor family background does not mean I have lost my senses. You are not very supportive and it is obvious you are discouraging my uncle from sending me back to school to further my education. Why? You want me to be your in-house babysitter to look after your children for twenty-four hours a day without making any plans for my own future."

***

A few months later Nneka still hadn't heard from Chief Uzodike about her schooling. Her uncle had continuously lied to her and made false promises. Despite everything, she was still determined and anxious to go back to college to further her education. She had wasted a lot of time waiting to hear from her obdurate uncaring uncle, so she decided to approach him face to face. She intended to tell him that since it seemed he was unable to fulfil his promises she had made up her mind to return to her parents in the village.

"Uncle, just to let you know I will soon be leaving to return to my parents. I have waited for so long to hear from you and you have failed to deliver. I have lost confidence in you and, therefore, I don't think it is advisable for me to stay in your home any longer and besides, I am not a servant. I feel that in the near future my parent's situation might improve if I am there to assist them with the farming. I have no friends here and I am devastated by the way you and your wife try to undermine me. Nothing seems to be working out for me, but why? It is all due to your apathy, so I am looking forward to being reunited with my poor parents in the village. You are unwilling to fulfil your promise, and you are no longer very supportive."

"This is an absolute disgrace Nneka. I am asking you, what the hell is your problem? Can't you just exercise a little patience and wait for few months? Do you think I have forgotten you?" her uncle asked.

"I honestly don't know," replied Nneka.

"I have not received the utmost respect from you since I brought you to my house. I have done my best trying to help you out as much as I can. You need to calm down and relax, and I promise you that you will soon be going back college to further your education, OK? Let me tell you, Nneka, if you continue to be so miserable and hostile towards me I am not going to assist you any further. Do I make myself clear to you now?"

"I understand, sir," replied Nneka.

"OK, get into the house and continue whatever you were doing in the kitchen for your aunt, and I really do understand your concerns," said Chief Uzodike.

***

Four days went by after Nneka's uncle had warned her of the consequences of her actions.

One afternoon her uncle returned from his office for his usual lunch break. Nneka was the only one at home, alone and busy in the kitchen preparing the meal for the entire family. Soon after eating his meal Chief Uzodike siezed his opportunity and asked Nneka for a short body massage. He requested Nneka to bring dusting powder while he lay horizontal on one of the sofas in his living room. With some urgency he asked Nneka to rub cream and powder all over his body, pretending that he was in excruciating pain – she had no idea he was faking it.

Nneka was fearful, knowing quite well it would lead to an ugly situation and repercussions if Oluchi came home. Despite her misgivings, she continued to massage all over her uncle's body, and suddenly he decided to disrobe, leaving his body entirely exposed. He immediately advised her to feel free to massage all over his body including his private parts without any panic, but the timid and vulnerable Nneka, who was absolutely shocked at seeing her respected and esteemed uncle completely naked for the first time in her life, couldn't believe what she was seeing. What was going on with her uncle, Chief Uzodike? Consenting to massage him would be better than refusing, which might result in a serious threat by her uncle. Nneka massaged him as he wished, then he demanded oral sex as he made more empty promises.

"Nneka, let me assure you that I am willing and prepared to offer you any assistance you need without hesitation, including getting you enrolled as soon as possible at the college to continue your studies. As we have both settled our differences I am now ready to listen to your problems, OK?

"OK," Nneka replied, showing no enthusiasm.

"You must guarantee me strict anonymity by keeping our sexual affairs secret. You must never tell anyone else about what we have done, all right?"

"Yes, I know, I am aware," Nneka replied, shaking her head.

Chief Uzodike forced his niece to have sexual intercourse with him. She was terrified, but at last found the words to speak to her overpowering uncle.

"I hope you are not mistaking me for your wife, Aunt Oluchi. I am your niece and not your wife. I am sure you are aware of what you have done to me. I hope you understand the severe consequences of your actions. If we are both discovered in the process of having an affair, either by your wife or someone else, what do you think will happen?"

"Hopefully, nothing will happen. Don't worry Nneka, we are not going to be caught or apprehended by anyone, OK? We are the only ones at home, so come here and please me."

Nneka, who was quite religious, was very upset when she was tricked into having unprotected sex. She was really pissed off and did not wish to speak to him.

"Nneka, see you soon and I'll speak to you later. I am really sorry, I am running out of time," said Chief Uzodike as he dressed quickly. "I guess you really enjoy my company. Please make sure you never tell anyone, and don't let me down, OK?"

Nneka couldn't believe what had happened and thought about trying to run away when her lover was making his way back to his office. As he drove away from the house he blew the horn twice and waved. She looked out through the window and saw her uncle departing. She was half naked with her hair tied up in a ponytail. There is no smoke without fire.

***

One week after Chief Uzodike's sexual liaison with Nneka, they became much closer. Chief Ozodike went to his office in the morning and returned each evening with expensive presents for Nneka, but nothing for his wife. Uncle and niece always shared jokes.

Oluchi noticed the intimate relationship blossoming between her husband and Nneka. She was quite sceptical at first, but she then became insanely jealous of Nneka, suggesting or thinking that something was dreadfully wrong. Yes, I can see the intimate relationship between my husband and Nneka now, she thought, shaking her head. It is absolute madness. I must go and speak to Nneka. I will see if I can persuade her to reveal what is going on between them. I have never seen such behaviour from my husband in the twenty years we have been married. She was perplexed and hurt.

"Nneka, will you come here now please because I need to find out something from you as a matter of urgency, OK?"

Nneka came to see her.

"Where is my husband?" enquired Oluchi.

"I don't know where he went," replied Nneka.

"There is a saying that when a man is dancing in the middle of the road without seeing anyone beating the drums for him, inevitably there must be someone hiding somewhere in the bush beating the drums for the person dancing," quoted Oluci.

"Aunt, I do not understand your proverb, please can you explain it to me?"

"I am asking you, Nneka whether you have started a relationship with your uncle, as I can see something fishy is going on between the two of you? Listen and let me tell you Nneka, you could get pregnant. There is no way a pregnant woman can hide her stomach from anyone after the first month of her pregnancy, so what about the eight months before she is due to give birth? It is absolutely impossible."

"I think you are talking rubbish, Aunt Oluchi. I can tell you that I have nothing to hide; therefore, you can go to any lengths you wish to find out the truth. Your husband, Chief Uzodike, is my uncle, and there is no way we could marry each other. It is forbidden according to our Igbo traditions and customs."

"Is that what you are trying to say? OK, I will wait until my husband comes back from his overseas business trip," said Oluchi.

Three

Chief Uzodike was overseas on business for almost two weeks. He returned home and found Nneka with bruises, scratches and scars all over her body, and suspected and feared she had been beaten by his wife. He immediately called Oluchi and demanded an immediate and urgent explanation, but she refused to say how Nneka had sustained her injuries.

"Listen Oluchi, there is no other person who can inflict such injuries except you. I know you tried to strangle Nneka and hit her about the head as a result of your jealousy. I predicted this before I left home for the business trip abroad."

Chief Uzodike asked Nneka to explain what his wife had done to her.

"Uncle, she kicked me, stamped on my face and spat on me."

Oluchi was very angry, feeling betrayed by her husband. She was too upset to speak to him, but yelled a warning at Nneka.

"Let me tell you, *stupid girl*, this is just the beginning and I will never stop bullying you until you learn how to respect your elders." She turned to her husband. "Since Nneka came into this house from the village she has been abusing and cursing me almost every day for no reason."

"What did she do to you, and what did you do to her?" asked Chief Uzodike.

"I told you earlier," she replied.

"And what did you tell me earlier?" asked Chief Uzodike.

"Nneka must learn how to behave. She has continued to ignore my rules in this house."

"I think *your* behaviour has become increasingly bizarre. I think you must calm down, Oluchi, and try to behave like a responsible housewife. You should try and treat Nneka as your own daughter and abstain from any act of callousness. Let me tell you, Oluchi my wife, being the head of this household it is my absolute priority and responsibility to get things right, which is why I am here to settle any dispute between you and my niece. Please let it be the first and last time you abuse her in this way. Do you want to kill the poor girl? What if she happened to die from the injuries she sustained as a result of your brutality? How would I explain it to her immediate family and besides, what would the elders say? Would they say that I brought Nneka from her parent's home to the city to be maltreated and killed? Please, I am warning you, Oluchi, stop beating Nneka, or one day you could face the serious consequences of your disgraceful actions."

Soon after Chief Uzodike had warned his wife he called to Nneka and asked her what she was doing.

"Sir, I am washing up plates in the kitchen."

"Will you get me a bottle of chilled Guinness from the fridge and bring it to me in my bedroom, OK?"

"Yes, sir," replied Nneka.

She took the beer for her uncle in his bedroom then waited to collect the cutlery to take back to the kitchen to continue the washing-up. He told her be seated.

"I want you to understand this, Nneka. Do you know why Oluchi was so angry and upset with you?"

"Yes Uncle," replied Nneka.

"Don't mind her. She is full of jealousy and became verbally aggressive, threatening you because she claimed that I love you more than her. Nneka can you please do me a favour?"

"What favour?" she enquired.

"Can we try that thing again today?"

"What?" she asked.

"Have you forgotten the unforgettable massage you gave me just four weeks ago when I came back home for my lunch break?"

"Yes, I do remember, but, Uncle, I have to say 'no' today. You must be joking; can't you see that my aunt is around and I believe she is listening to our private conversation from behind the kitchen door. I am not willing to be involved in another confrontation with her. As you know quite well she is a quarrelsome and frightful woman, and I can't argue back as I have to be abjectly subservient to her. Can't you forget about having a body massage today, and postpone it until tomorrow when you come back home for your lunch? I will give you a nice relaxing body massage then, OK? I know your tactics quite well; you request a body massage, but afterwards you expect sexual intercourse, which is becoming a habit."

Listen Nneka, I am only asking for a quick body massage I can assure you. How can I have sexual intercourse with you when my wife is around? Do you think I am sex mad?"

"Despite being sexually attracted to you, I am sick and tired of this irresponsible, obscene and salacious behaviour of yours," said Nneka. "I don't want to be brutally beaten up persistently by Aunt Oluchi. I really don't understand why you keep asking me for a massage when your wife is here to offer you whatever you ask or demand from her. Please, why can't you go and approach your wife instead of trying to abuse me physically and mentally almost every day? Aunt Oluchi is your wife as well as your property," she added. "Can I ask you one question?"

"Yes you can, go on, ask me a question." said Chief Uzodike.

"Uncle, are you afraid of discussing sexual excitement with your wife? Do you need someone to help you to speak to your wife on your behalf?"

"I am absolutely not and will never be afraid of my own wife," replied Chief Uzodike. "I do not find it awkward to ask Oluchi for a body massage or sexual intercourse, we have both quite often. The fact is that with her it is extremely difficult to have that sensual stimulation; however, with you I believe I can regain the excitement that I no longer have with my wife. I am very pleased that you are here to show me the romantic gestures that actually make me feel erogenous."

"Sorry Uncle, I can't really help you out with a body massage today. I have made it absolutely clear to you before that I don't want any further conflict with your wife and besides, I am not a whore. I am going back to the kitchen to help my aunt to prepare the evening meal. No doubt by now she is thinking about what has been going inside the bedroom between you and me, as I am supposed to be assisting her in the kitchen. I am sorry I have to go now."

"Come on, relax and don't worry about my Oluchi," he said. Nneka's uncle went on to reassure her that he was the head of the household and he would take personal responsibility for whatever happened to her. "Don't forget that I am only asking you for a body massage and not sexual intercourse."

"Yes Uncle, but I know all about your sly tactics. Please don't think I am ungrateful because you brought me to your house, but let me tell you this is not what I came for. I am here for a purpose and you, having been unable to keep your promises, now want to exploit me sexually. Don't forget that I come from a Christian background and know that any such act is immoral, unethical and disreputable."

"Listen Nneka, I am not trying to exploit you by asking you for a quick body massage, which I know is wrong, and I do understand your anger, as none of the promises I made have been met. I am sincerely sorry for any pain that I have caused. You are now free to go and help your aunt to prepare the dinner in the kitchen, OK? Please don't reveal anything to her," added Chief Uzodike.

"Yes Uncle," said Nneka.

On her way to the kitchen, Nneka was met by Oluchi, who asked her where she had been for so long. She had been very busy in the kitchen preparing the evening meal alone without any assistance from her niece.

"I was in the house with my uncle in his bedroom, talking. He invited me into his room for a chat," Nneka replied.

"Nneka, when did you start chatting with my husband and, by the way, who gave you permission to enter our bedroom without my knowledge?" she shouted. "*Chimoo*! Yes, I said it earlier on that this girl would one day take over my position in this house. *Chimoo*!" she shouted hysterically. She placed her hands on her head and made her way out of the kitchen saying, "My two eyes are seeing my two ears."

Oluchi went to her next door neighbour to complain about Nneka's behaviour towards her husband, but unfortunately nobody was at home, so she returned to the kitchen to continue cooking the evening meal.

Nneka was very frightened and shaken, and timorous to face her aunt due to her cruel and unkind behaviour. She was astounded to see her aunt going crazy because she went into her uncle's bedroom without Oluchi's authorisation. She had not expected to encounter such ill-mannered and ungracious behaviour from her aunt. She was speechless as she stood and watched her screaming like a mad dog.

"I hope you are not trying to seduce my husband," yelled Oluchi.

"*No*, I am not a tart or shameless as you think. Your husband, Chief Uzodike, is my uncle and I see nothing wrong in going to his bedroom without your consent or knowledge. By the way, has anyone reported any act of sexual encounter between your husband and myself?" she asked.

"How many times have I warned you about going to my husband's bedroom? Just to inform you, if you are not aware, my husband is just an uncle to you and never a husband, OK? You have no permission whatsoever to visit or go near our bedroom."

"As I have told you already, I have done nothing wrong by going to your husband's bedroom and by the way, I did not force my way into the bedroom without his consent or knowledge; he was the one who asked *me* for a favour."

"What favour?" asked Oluchi.

"He asked me to collect a bottle of Guinness from the fridge and take it to his bedroom." "So, my husband was the one who invited you to his bedroom?"

"Yes. Aunt Oluchi, I just told you that. Why can't you try to listen attentively before reacting so angrily?"

"You must learn your boundaries in this house and besides, you should not take everything for granted."

***

Nneka was really scared to face her aunt sometime later. She finally plucked up enough courage to go into the kitchen in the hope that maybe Oluchi have forgiven her. She had no idea her aunt had been planning how to punish her. As soon as Nneka entered the kitchen to help with the cooking and washing-up, she was slapped, kicked and thrown to the ground.

Chief Uzodike heard Nneka's loud cries coming from the kitchen, so he immediately left his bedroom and hurried to see what had happened. On arrival he saw Nneka crying, her dress soaked with liquid from a pan of hot grease and water that had been poured over her body by his wife. Chief Uzodike was extremely angry.

"Oluchi, how dare you pour hot liquid all over Nneka. What did she do to you that would warrant this maltreatment of her in such a brutal and inhumane manner? Do you want to kill my niece because she visits my bedroom without your permission? By the way, maybe *you* need permission from me before coming to my bedroom?"

"Why?" Oluchi screamed. "I *am* your wife!"

"Nneka is my niece," said Chief Uzodike. "She did not come to my bedroom to play or have fun. I invited her and she has every right to come and go freely without any aggravation. What is your problem? Why can't you allow poor Nneka to live in peace?"

"*My* problem is *your* problem."

"No Oluchi my wife, I think you have it all wrong. Please stop tormenting Nneka. By the way, she is not your daughter, so you have no right whatsoever to mistreat her so badly," said Chief Uzodike.

He told Nneka to go and have a bath. He was absolutely miserable and frustrated when he realised his tactics to seduce his niece were not working. He persisted in asking her for an enduring body massage, but she refused and returned to the kitchen to placate Oluchi by helping her to prepare the evening meal.

***

Nneka's bondage, subjugation and servitude continued, and she lost the desire to enrol at college to pursue her studies. Her hard-hearted aunt had not given her any opportunity to leave her uncle's home since her arrival from the village.

One fateful afternoon Oluchi sent Nneka to the market for the first time since her arrival, to buy extra food. She was not given any money for transport, but was told to walk along the track to the market that was miles away from her uncle's home. After walking for four hours Nneka finally reached the market where she purchased the foodstuff Oluchi required. On her way back home, exhausted by the long journey, she was abducted by an armed gangster and immediately taken captive.

***

Oluchi waited for a long time without seeing Nneka return home. She suddenly became quite apprehensive and worried, wondering if something had gone wrong. Nneka had left home without a mobile phone or any form of communication in case of an emergency. Oluchi had prohibited her from using one, so she had no idea of her whereabouts. She shouted loudly and shook her head twice saying:

"No, something is not right. I must go to the market to speak to my friend Ngozi, who sells gari there. I told Nneka to go and buy some foodstuff from her."

When Oluchi arrived at the market, she was met by her friend, Ngozi, who asked her why she was looking worn out and scrawny, wearing dirty clothes and coming barefoot to the market.

"I hope all is well with you," said Ngozi.

"Ngozi, have you seen my maid Nneka at all today?" asked Oluchi. "I actually sent her to buy foodstuff from you-"

"Who is your maid?" Ngozi interrupted her. "I honestly don't think I have met her before."

"I think you met Nneka sometime ago when you came to my house for my husband's birthday party."

"When was that?" asked Ngozi.

"It was only six months ago when my husband, Chief Uzodike, had his lavish birthday party."

"Oh yes, I remember her now. You told me you would never allow your maid out of your house, so did you decide to change your mind today and send her to buy from the market?" asked Ngozi. "What was going on in your mind? Have you forgotten that she could easily be abducted, as she is so young and naive? I honestly haven't seen her in my shop today. I advise you to start looking for her now, before it gets too late."

"I wouldn't know where to start."

"Let me warn you about Nneka's parents. They will be so vengeful, especially Nneka's father, Anaeke, who will ensure that you pay the ultimate price if anything happens to his daughter. Remember this quote, 'It is better to start looking for a lost black goat in the broad daylight before it gets dark, because when it gets dark it will be very difficult to find due to its colour'. I am blaming you Oluchi; how foolish you have been to send Nneka to the market on her own without someone who knows the market well. Have you forgotten how dangerous Lagos city market is? If I was you, I would contact the police immediately."

Oluchi told her friend she had no idea where Nneka would be, and asked Ngozi where she should start looking for her.

"You should be ashamed of yourself, asking me where to start looking. Oluchi, do you know where the police station is? Go to the police station and report her missing, so they can start searching for her, instead of wasting your bloody time asking me ludicrous questions," said Ngozi. "What if she has been kidnapped? What will you do?"

"I don't know what to do, and I am thinking about what could have happened to Nneka, my friend," Oluchi replied.

"By the way, how did you send Nneka to the market? Did you give her money for the bus fare, or did you ask someone to give her a lift? Please tell me, I just want to know," said Ngozi.

"Ngozi, to be honest I didn't give Nneka any transport money, but told her to walk to and from the market."

"Oluchi, why are you so heartless? If Nneka was your own daughter, would you ask her to walk to and from the market alone? Remember, if you do something bad to someone's daughter, vice versa, someone must do the same to your daughter, bear that in mind. Just cross your fingers and pray that she returns home safe and sound. Hopefully nothing has happened to her, otherwise you will be held accountable by her parents."

"It never crossed my mind that something dreadful could happen to her," said Oluchi.

"Come on, Oluchi, please stop saying you did not think something could happen. I don't believe what you say any more. You know quite well that you were trying to punish the poor girl and want her dead. This is not how you should treat your maid. I think you should go and learn from other women who are in a similar situation as you."

"Thank you for your advice, I must go now," said Oluchi.

"OK, take care of yourself and please try to find out Nneka's whereabouts as soon as possible."

"Yes, Ngozi I will try my best, bye."

***

Soon after Oluchi reported Nneka's disappearance to the police, Chief Uzodike was informed about what had happened by some of his close friends and neighbours. He left his office immediately to rush home, and was very angry with his wife.

"How did this happen? Please, give me an explanation, Oluchi," he said.

Oluchi explained everything to her husband.

"This is absolute madness, what do I do now? What am I going to tell Nneka's parents, and where do I start to search for Nneka?" Chief Uzodike questioned, distraught. "I honestly fear that her captors might decide to rape and kill her, or they might contact us with a demand for a huge sum of ransom money. I am not worried about the ransom money; all I want now is to have Nneka returned home unhurt. The lack of communication is going to make it more difficult to track down her whereabouts."

Oluchi told her husband that it was all her fault and she was truly sorry for all the mistakes she had made. Chief Uzodike assured his wife that if Nneka wasn't found unharmed he would burn down the family home.

Nneka was nowhere to be found, so Chief Uzodike, who hadn't spoken to Nneka's parents since her arrival in the city, hinted at going to the village to inform them of the dreadful circumstances.

"As it stands now, there is no need to keep it a secret. This is everybody's problem, and I am contemplating going to inform her parents of the situation."

"No, there is no need to do that at this early stage of the investigation; it would make the situation far worse. It would have a devastating impact on Nneka's family," said Oluchi.

***

The hunt for Nneka continued.

Chief Uzodike was under intense pressure, rushing around trying to unearth any indication or clue that might lead to Nneka's whereabouts. His mobile phone rang twice with the number withheld, then shortly afterwards it rang again for the third time. He answered hurriedly.

"Hello, may I know who is speaking?" he enquired.

"Am I speaking to Chief Uzodike?"

"Yes, who are you?"

"I am calling to let you know that we are currently holding your maid, Nneka, hostage. She is well and in a secret location. Do you have a pen and paper handy?"

"Yes."

"OK Chief, this is our bank account number and we would like you to write it down. Listen very carefully to the numbers. We give you seven days from now to pay the sum of ten million naira. If you fail to do so it will result in your maid, Nneka, being killed within the next ten days. Please take note, Chief Uzodike. Once our ransom demand is met your maid will be set free."

Chief Uzodike, full of consternation, immediately went to speak to Oluchi about the phone call.

"I am very pleased to hear some news of Nneka at last, but my main concern now is where I will get the sum of ten million naira within seven days as requested by the kidnappers."

"Listen, my loving husband Uzodike, do whatever it takes to ensure that you give the ransom demand to these deplorable individuals before the deadline elapses. If you have decided to go ahead in selling off every valuable possession we own, including our residential home, I am absolutely in support in order to ensure that Nneka regains her freedom without any further delay."

"Yes, I do understand that Oluchi, but where do I start? Do I have to first embark on selling off both my valuable properties, and my one and only ostentatious pleasurable sports car?"

"Listen, you can start wherever you like and moreover, dispose of whatever is necessary, sell me, you are free to do so. I have no problem at all with that."

Chief Uzodike could not believe what his wife had suggested and told her that he certainly would not consider her proposition. He said that if the worst came to the worst he would even resort to begging his closest friends for financial assistance to gain the ransom money, something he would find extremely difficult.

Oluchi began to cry when she realised all their admired and cherished personal property, such as her husband's costly and magnificent sports car as well as their stylish and contemporary family mansion had to be sold in order to accumulate the cash to pay for the ransom demand. They were also running out of time.

"I hope in the near future that you and I will be able to find another marvellous mansion like this one," said Oluchi, through her tears.

"Yes I know Oluchi, my wife, it is so painful, but what can I do? The most important thing is to get Nneka out of captivity."

***

Some days later the sum of ten million naira was transferred into the bandits' account.

Soon afterwards, Nneka was set free unhurt, after spending fourteen days in captivity. On returning home, she was reunited with and welcomed by a large delighted crowd, family friends and neighbours of Chief Uzodike, who were waiting anxiously to see her.

Oluchi, who had been the cause of Nneka's abduction, shouted joyously and apologised to Nneka by saying:

"I am very sorry, Nneka, it was my frivolous mistake, and I promise it will never happen again. Please forgive me."

They both hugged each other.

Four

Two months later, Chief Uzodike and his wife Oluchi decided to send Nneka back to college to further her education. Oluchi was sorry for the many years of resentment she had felt, the distress and suffering she had inflicted on Nneka and how she had treated her like a slave - a cause for celebration.

Nneka was offered a place to study at the Federal Government College Ekponi, through the help and support of her uncle, Chief Uzodike. Nneka was delighted and could not hide her powerful emotions upon hearing she had met the college's admission criteria and her fees would be paid by her uncle.

"This is a really a dream come true. I am absolutely delighted and looking forward to telling my parents, especially Mum, who will be so thrilled, joyful and proud," said a happy Nneka.

"Nneka, I believe this is the most effective time for you to be able to fulfil your ambition and also to achieve your full potential," said her uncle.

"I always told you that there is no age limit to go to college; I went when I was twenty-five years old. I want you to understand that it is never too late for you to achieve whatever you desire in as much as you are strongly motivated to succeed. There is a saying that he who laughs last laughs longest."

He instructed Oluchi to take Nneka to the market to purchase all that she needed for college including the uniform, sandals, textbooks etc. He also told his wife to give whatever cash was left over to Nneka as school pocket money. He asked Nneka to make sure she spent her pocket money very wisely then advised her to be honourable and persevere in carrying out her studies. He warned her to refrain from any act of boisterous behaviour and to be beware of the college gang culture.

"I will do whatever it takes to ensure that your school fees are paid on time every term," he promised. "I advise you to be industrious and shrewd in dealing with your studies, so that at the end of your time at college you will graduate with flying colours."

Chief Uzodike gave Nneka strict instructions that she should never travel to the college alone for whatever reason, adding that she would be dropped off at the college every morning and picked up every evening by Emma, his private chauffeur.

Nneka and Oluchi left for the market to purchase all that Nneka required for her college life.

"Nneka, I know I have offended you in the past, but please let us bury the hatchet. I have so much good advice for you, but I am not going to say a word to you to avoid further confrontation. Just to inform you in advance, you will still be expected to continue your domestic chores for me."

The next day Nneka commenced her studies at the Federal Government College Ekponi. She was much more relaxed, and really impressed with her new college. She acknowledged that her chosen curriculum was fantastic, and was glad that everything was going as well as expected. She became accustomed to waking up early in the morning to get ready to travel to the college with her uncle's chauffeur.

***

It was not long before Nneka suffered another setback when her uncle resumed his sexual infatuation with her. She suspected something was wrong when she began to feel strange and started to vomit each morning. She decided to approach her uncle's wife to alert her of her condition when she came to the conclusion that she might be pregnant.

Oluchi had just returned from her home village after visiting her gravely ill mother, who had been admitted to the hospital. Nneka was very reluctant to disclose any sexual act between herself and her uncle in order to avoid damaging her uncle's reputation; however, she plucked up the courage to insinuate that Chief Uzodike was the father of her unborn child.

"Aunt Oluchi, I am pregnant."

"Shut up and remain quiet now," said Oluchi. "Who is the father?"

"My uncle impregnated me," replied Nneka.

"Which of your uncles got you pregnant?" asked Oluchi.

"Aunt Oluchi, I want you to tell me how many uncles I have here in the city apart from your husband, Chief Uzodike."

"I don't know, you tell me, Nneka," replied Oluchi.

"Anyway, just to let you know, if you are not aware, I have no other uncle here in this city apart from your husband. Anyway, he is the person who has made me pregnant."

"Are you sure what you are saying is true?"

"Yes, Aunt Oluchi," Nneka replied.

"Nneka, when did you sleep with my husband? Please feel free to explain to me."

"It happened one weekend when you travelled to the village to attend the burial ceremony of one of your relatives who had just passed away. We were the only ones at home and I never expected such a foolish act from my uncle. He started to ask me for a favour and all of a sudden he made me arrange the water for his evening bath. After his bath he came out of the washroom and asked me to massage him all over his body with body lotion. Afterwards he told me to shut the door and turn off the lights. He suddenly grabbed my breasts, squeezed them and demanded that I removed my underwear. That was when I realised he was desperate to have sexual intercourse with me. One thought came into my mind, therefore, I hastily asked my uncle twice:

"What if I get pregnant by you? What will you do and what will you tell your wife and my parents?"

My uncle promised that I would not get pregnant and that he would use a contraceptive. I asked him if he really knew about the consequences of asking me for sex, and he said he was fully aware. Aunt, I questioned him and told him that he didn't know anything about the consequences of his actions, otherwise he would not have asked me, his own blood niece, to engage in sexual intercourse. He knew it was wrong, but it didn't stop him from having his way with me," revealed Nneka.

Shortly after Nneka's revelation, Oluchi burst into tears.

"*Chimoo bia lele anya mu awuru nti mu* (my God come and look my eyes have seen my two ears)," she wailed. "I have never seen or heard such an abomination in all my life. God forbid. I feel like heading to the village to inform the elders right now, but it is too early to speculate, therefore, I must wait until I have spoken to my husband. I am not going to jump to conclusions now. If this is the case Nneka, we will soon be going to the hospital to get a pregnancy test done. This is a serious allegation that requires to be treated with desperation," said Oluchi.

Oluchi decided to take Nneka to the hospital immediately to have her urine tested in order to prove the authenticity of her allegation. If the result of the test confirmed she was pregnant, she would do whatever it took to make sure she brandished her so-called husband a rapist.

"What are your intentions? Do you have any plans for yourself now? Do you intend to get married to your uncle and become his wife?" Oluchi asked her niece.

"No, Aunt Oluchi, please don't say that; there is no way I would marry my blood uncle."

"If you are not planning to get married, why did you agree to engage in sexual intercourse with him?"

"Aunt Oluchi, it was an imprudent mistake," replied Nneka.

"Can I tell you what you obviously don't know? For you to have an affair with a married man out of wedlock is regarded as an abomination, and that is the case now. The only way to restore your credibility, righteousness and integrity is to get married to your uncle."

"You must both take the responsibility for the disgrace, shame and humiliation caused, and besides, your husband has ruined my life," said Nneka.

"I blame you Nneka, all this is your own fault. How many times have I warned you to stay away from my husband, after I noticed you were so close to him? Despite my early warnings you kept ignoring me. How many times have I caught you chatting with my husband in his bedroom? I repeatedly warned you to desist from going into his bedroom, but you refused to listen to me. Some time ago I suspected that both of you were having an affair and I approached you about that, but you emphatically and vigorously denied any wrongdoing. I honestly don't know how to explain how I am feeling right now, and you have let me and your parents down after all the sacrifices your mother made in order to see that you came to this city. You have failed to realise you come from a disadvantaged background and you should have put more effort into trying to meet all your challenges. When you left your parent's home, you actually left promising them and your two siblings a better life through your endeavours. You said you would pay them back, especially your mum for all she gave up for you. Now all you can do is return to your parents with an unwanted pregnancy, not even with a stranger but with your own blood uncle as a result of your vulgarity, discourtesy and incivility."

Oluchi continued to explain that she had tried all she could to help Nneka out in any way she could, but now felt she was trying to undermine her by trying to jeopardise her marriage.

"You have ruined my family and at the same time taken over my authority in this household as the overall commander. On top of everything, what upsets me most is that you have been perpetually and systematically alluring my husband into sexual activity with you. Nneka, when you first came into this home from your parent's home, I offered you impeccable hospitality that you would never forget for the rest of your life. I always ensured that I gave you whatever you asked me for and, concerning your studies, I tried hard to enrol you into one of the leading colleges in the city, but wasn't successful. Nneka, you have shown no concern for my feelings and as a consequence, you have left me devastated after all I have done for you. You pay me back by putting my family into turmoil. I have never seen such an ugly situation like this before in my life. It is an outcry for a niece to become pregnant by her own blood uncle, you are absolutely incorrigible. I will move out of my matrimonial home with my children, so that you will be comfortable to relax with my husband. I am not going to fight with my husband over such a nonentity as you, who came from a poverty-stricken background. I have been let down by both of you and feel humiliated and betrayed in every way."

"Aunt Oluchi, I am so sorry for any pain that I have caused, and I apologise for my monstrous mistakes. However, you must not put all the blame on me alone; you must blame your husband for pressurising me to commit sexual perversion. As a consequence I have lost all my credibility, and also my reputation has been tarnished and damaged. I am also destitute after spending more than seven years as a housemaid for you, with no hopeful future, no money and without any formal qualifications. I am so frustrated and demoralised; this is an absolute disgrace, not only to me, but to my entire family. I can't imagine what I was thinking, having come from a very decent Christian background where immoral conduct is not tolerated by my strict and inspirational parents. I don't know how I am going to explain it to my parents, especially my mum, Rosemary, who sacrificed so much in order to see that my mission of relocating to the city was accomplished. My dad, Anaeke, a strict hard working and easy to anger individual, sold whatever he could in order to pay for my school fees, but I had to give up my schooling due to my parent's financial predicament. My mum and dad expected me to be a well-mannered and obedient girl. This is causing me a great deal of concern, and I fear the consequences, as I am about to return to my parent's home."

"Nneka, I know that you are at fault. I did complain of your bizarre behaviour towards my husband, Chief Uzodike, and also warned you to desist from any act of indignity as well as to refrain from wearing any kind of provocative attire that could cause or evoke sexual desire on his part, but you did not listen and did not heed my warning. This is medicine after death. The fact that you had no money has already been forgotten and I feel betrayed and cheated by my husband, your uncle, also I blame both of you."

Shortly after, it was made known by the medical practitioner that Nneka was pregnant and it emerged that her uncle, Chief Uzodike, was responsible for her pregnancy. Chief Uzodike admitted the fact, expressed remorse and pleaded for anonymity from his wife Oluchi and Nneka in order to avoid damaging his reputation. He assured Nneka that she would receive a lump sum - hush money - and offered her another incentive in the form of financial stability. He pledged to purchase her a stylish and contemporary bungalow or house.

"It is imperative that I search for a decent and responsible person to be your husband, but only if you agree to the following conditions. The first is that you must never tell anyone, including your parents, that I got you pregnant, and secondly you must never mention to anyone, whatever happens, that I am the biological father of your unborn baby. Emma is my private chauffeur, and I am going to ask him to accept the responsibility as a favour to me. There is no cause for alarm. Emma has huge respect for me and besides, he is like a blood cousin to me," said Chief Uzodike.

He went to tell his wife of his decision.

"Are you out of your mind, my husband Chief Uzodike? How dare you, and how could you do this to your own blood niece? How could you expect Nneka to lie about her pregnancy, while everyone in this neighbourhood is aware of what is going on between you and Nneka at the moment?"

"How do you know what everyone in this neighbourhood is aware of, Oluchi?" asked Chief Uzodike.

"Because yesterday I met Chinwe in the market, who anxiously came to ask me if what she was hearing about my husband and his maid, Nneka, was true. Had my husband got his maid pregnant? I told her that it was true that my husband had impregnated our housemaid."

"Who told her in the first place?" asked Chief Uzodike.

"I honestly don't know," replied Oluchi.

"By the way, who is Chinwe?"

"Are you asking me who she is, don't you know Chief Agumba's second wife?"

"Is she the loquacious and troublesome woman who engages in a shameful street fight with Agumba almost every day? It nearly killed him a few months ago when she held him captive for four days and threatened to kill him. Luckily he was rescued by one of their next door neighbours." He put his hands on his head and shouted, "*Chimoo*, I am in big trouble! There is no need to pretend if nearly everyone already knows, and I believe through this treacherous woman, Agumba's wife, those who were not aware of the situation will soon be aware. I wonder who narrated the story to her?" asked chief.

"I have already told you I don't know," Oluchi replied. "Let me ask you, Chief Uzodike, if you are not going to admit responsibility for

Nneka's pregnancy, who do you expect to be responsible? You might be better off if you married Nneka instead of searching for someone to take over the responsibility."

"Earlier on, what did I say to you?" asked Chief Uzodike.

"Remind me, I honestly cannot remember."

"I am going to arrange for a marriage of convenience between Emma and Nneka as I have mentioned before. Who else can I possibly ask to pretend to be the biological father of my unborn baby? Calm down, Oluchi, and relax your mind. That is not a big issue and hopefully will come to an end soon."

"OK, if that is the case I am pleased to hear about it from you," said Oluchi.

"I am going to organise an arranged marriage as soon as possible between Emma, my private chauffeur, and Nneka. I am going to force Emma to claim that he is the biological father of Nneka's unborn baby. As you are quite aware, Emma is so destitute, he struggles to make ends meet and he is under intense pressure from his landlord, who has threatened to evict him at any time. Furthermore, he has mounting pressure from his parents, who are constantly asking for money to pay for his sibling's school fees. Owing to his present financial predicament I don't think Emma has any choice other than to agree to execute the plan for me. I am quite convinced that Emma knows what the consequences will be if he fails me by refusing to marry Nneka; his job as my private chauffeur would be terminated." said Chief Uzodike.,

Nneka had stood quietly listening to her uncle and aunt's conversation, and she was incensed by his suggestion.

"Uncle, are you saying that I should marry that bigoted, indigent and wearisome chauffeur of yours called Emma? Sorry, I will not marry him. He is certainly not the type of man that I am looking forward to marrying. I will not agree to this, over my dead body. This is absolutely ridiculous. Instead of marrying Emma, who is more than twenty years older than me, I prefer to return to my parent's home in the village. Emma is also insolvent and he comes from an underprivileged family background. He is a Muslim and comes from a traditional Muslim family, while I am a Christian, who comes from a very strict and devoted Christian family. This is absolutely impossible, and there is no way we should get married to each other," said Nneka indignantly.

"I understand that, Nneka, but I want you to understand this too. I am not making the choice of a man or husband for you, but I am trying to figure out a solution that would be ideal for us both. I am trying to protect you from being bullied or ostracised by your parents, and also to avoid myself being named and shamed, which would damage my reputation. Do you hope that I will be shamed and humiliated by both your parents and your elders?" asked Chief Uzodike.

"Absolutely not," replied Nneka.

"So, for obvious reasons I am making sure that I do whatever it takes to ensure that no one hears about it. I know quite well what I did to you was wrong. I committed an abomination by having an affair with you and besides, if the rumour spreads further afield, severe physical punishment would be inevitable."

"I understand that, Uncle, but how can you force me to get married to Emma? This is absolutely against my beliefs. How can he look after me financially when he is in a financial predicament?" asked Nneka.

"Chill out and stop beating about the bush Nneka. I am going to ensure that you are both well looked after by me, and in addition I am going to provide you with some cash, but make sure you spend your money wisely.

"You can say whatever you want to say, Uncle, but I will not change my mind and will not accept any financial incentive from you, period."

"My husband," said Oluchi, "you should understand the needs of others. I know this lewd act is causing you a great deal of concern and you must therefore blame yourself. This is your own fault. Why did you sleep with Nneka? You should be ashamed of yourself. Have you any idea how I feel about all this?"

"Yes, I have," replied Chief.

"I am deeply sad and left devastated and humiliated just because of your senseless act. Despite that, I have chosen to remain calm just for the sake of my children," said Oluchi.

***

Later on that day, Oluchi tried to persuade Nneka to reconsider, clinch the deal hastily and marry Emma as promptly as possible. She asked Nneka to help in any way she could.

"I know it is detestable to you, and realise that it is going to be extremely laborious, but I advise you to play the game adeptly and agree to tie the knot with Emma," said Oluchi. "I know that money is not the only thing holding you back, but I can assure you that I am going to offer you both the practical and financial support needed if you agree to marry him."

"Yes, Aunt," replied Nneka, pretending to agree with her.

"Well done, Nneka, and thank you for letting me know," said Oluchi.

***

Oluchi went to find her husband to tell him the good news.

"Where are you?" she called out.

"I am here." he replied.

"Where?"

"I am taking a shower," said Chief Uzodike.

Oluchi hurried upstairs to meet her husband in the washroom.

"Listen Chief, Nneka asked me to tell you that she has agreed to marry your private chauffeur, Emma."

"What good news. Thank you so much, Oluchi." said Chief Uzodike.

Immediately after receiving the good news, Chief Ozudike asked his private chauffeur to come to him for an urgent briefing.

"I have not spoken to Nneka's parents for a long time. I am asking you now to go and inform them that we are coming for the traditional marriage between you and Nneka in about two weeks' time," said Chief Uzodike.

Emma was sent out immediately to go and meet Nneka's parents in the village and also to negotiate a convenient date for the forthcoming traditional marriage ceremony between himself and Nneka. He was also asked to obtain from Nneka's elders the list of the mandatory items required for the traditional marriage.

***

When Emma arrived in the village he was met by Nneka's parents, Anaeke and his wife, Rosemary.

"Who are you, my son?" asked Anaeke.

"I am Mr Emma Onwuna Ndu (which literally means 'death and life')", replied Emma.

"And where do you come from, Mr. Onwuna Ndu?" asked Anaeke.

"I come from the beautiful city of Lagos."

"Yes, I have heard about the stunning city of Lagos, but I have never been there. My daughter, Nneka, and her uncle, Chief Uzodike, reside in the city," said Anaeke.

"Yes, I know your daughter and her uncle. I am here today to inform you that Nneka and I are planning to get married soon. Your daughter is to have our baby, which is why I was sent by Chief Uzodike to negotiate a suitable date for the traditional marriage ceremony to take place here in your compound. I would also like to have a comprehensive list from you and your elders of all the items needed."

"*Fantastic!*" exclaimed Anaeke. "Well done, you are highly esteemed and it's nice to meet you. Sorry to ask you Emma, please, what do you do for a living?"

"I am a chauffeur," he replied.

"I hope you two love each other?"

"Yes we do," said Emma.

"You and my daughter look remarkably similar, and if that's the case my wife and I are both happy to accept your hand in marriage to our beautiful daughter, Nneka. Listen to us, Emma, you will receive the list of things you are requesting from us as soon as possible, and we trust that you will find this arrangement satisfactory." Later on Anaeke and Rosemary added, "We are delighted to support you in your forthcoming traditional marriage ceremony, and would like thank you once again. We are looking forward to the big day, and have a safe journey back home."

In response, Emma praised and thanked Anaeke and Rosemary.

"Thank you very much indeed, and it is lovely to meet both of you. What wonderful and fantastic in-laws you will be. You are both very supportive and helpful. My mum always said to me to make sure I always do whatever my in-laws say, but that I should always be friends with my wife and never my in-laws, or they could ruin my marriage, especially mother-in-laws, who are so powerful, narrow minded and largely to blame in matrimonial disputes. The success of your marriage is in the hands of your in-laws."

Emma was given the comprehensive list of all the items to be purchased for the traditional marriage ceremony then he returned to the city to report to his boss, Chief Uzodike. Shortly after arriving home, he was met by Chief Uzodike and Oluchi, who collected the list from him. Oluchi hurriedly went to the market to buy all the listed items.

Five

One week later all the necessary arrangements for the traditional marriage ceremony between Emma and Nneka were complete.

Everyone travelled to Nneka's hometown with Chief Uzodike, his wife, Oluchi, Emma and Nneka. There were friends and neighbours as well as relatives from both sides.

On arrival they were met by a large crowd that had gathered to witness the Igba Nkwu Nwanyi ceremony. Both young and old were wearing spectacular agbada. When all the invited guests were seated in the front of Anaeke's house, he stood with his wife to greet them.

"*Igbo nma nwu, Igbo kwe num, Kwe zoo nu,*" he said. "I am happy today that my daughter Nneka is getting married to the man she loves. I would like to take this opportunity to thank everyone, especially my in-laws, Chief Uzodike and his wife, our amiable traditional ruler, Eze Agu, and his red cap Chiefs, also those of you who have come from far and wide to witness my daughter's traditional marriage ceremony - you are all welcome."

The traditional ruler of the host village, Eze Agu, then praised Nneka's father, Anaeke, describing him as a 'great son of his land'.

"In fact, you and your daughter, Nneka, make us proud," he added.

The traditional ruler requested the breaking of the Kola nut, whereupon he asked anyone present from the villages of Eluoha, Aloma and Umuoma to please come forward to collect one Kola nut.

"As tradition demands, marriage in Igbo land is not recognised until the bride price is paid," he said.

He hurriedly directed Anaeke to go and ask his daughter to come forward and collect a glass of palm wine from him to serve to her husband-to-be for him to drink before they could proceed further.

Anaeke quickly went to the kitchen to look for Nneka, but she was not there. His wife, Rosemary, was with two female stewards who had been hired by Chief Uzodike and his wife Oluchi to cook food for the guests.

"Rosemary, where is our daughter, Nneka?" enquired Anaeke.

"She has just gone to the toilet."

Nneka returned to the kitchen, was given the message and rushed off to meet the traditional ruler, who briskly cautioned her not to be shy.

"Yes, Nnayi Onye Eze."

"Take this glass of palm wine from me now and give it to whoever is your husband-to-be. He must drink and then you both come forward for a blessing."

"Yes, Nnayi Onye Eze," Nneka replied.

As tradition demands, one of the rules of a traditional marriage engagement in Igbo land is that the bride must bestow upon the bridegroom a glass of palm wine to drink to show that they both love each other, and to indicate that they both consent to the traditional marriage engagement.

Nneka collected the glass of palm wine from the traditional ruler; however, she refused to take it tor the groom, instead she gave the glass of palm wine to her father, Anaeke, which indicated that something had gone wrong and there was some distrust. She put her hands on her head and spoke.

"I have something to say, council of elders."

"Let us hear what you have to say," the traditional ruler requested, looking worried.

Nneka went on to disclose that it was not a real marriage.

"It is an arranged marriage, plotted by Chief Uzodike as a cover-up. How can I get married to a drifter, who is over twenty years older than me, someone I do not love, and someone who is not even the biological father of my unborn baby?"

"Who is the father if not Emma?" Eze Agu asked.

"I do not know who he is, ask my uncle, Chief Uzodike," replied Nneka.

"If the gentleman who was to be your future husband is not the biological father of your unborn baby as you have just disclosed, who *is* the biological father?"

"My uncle is the biological father of my unborn baby," replied Nneka.

"Who is your uncle?" asked the traditional ruler.

"Chief Uzodike."

"This is an abomination! This farce of a marriage ceremony plot between Nneka and Emma Onuru-Na ndu, hatched by ingenious Chief Uzodike, has been suspended, and I would like to ask everyone present to go home. Nneka will neither marry against her will nor be forced to marry someone she dislikes. She will remain in this village with her parents until she gives birth, and thereafter her new baby will be entrusted to her uncle to be cared for as a consequence of his misdeed. There is no cause for alarm, but I am afraid we are not going to accept the baby, and that is conclusive."

After being exposed by Nneka, Chief Uzodike made a quick exit from the proceedings, along with his wife Oluchi and his chauffeur Emma. He was nowhere to be found by the elders who tried to reach out to him.

Anaeke was very upset.

"What can I say? I am absolutely shocked and speechless."

Rosemary was distressed and in tears.

"How could my own blood brother, Chief Uzodike, act so treacherously towards his own blood niece? I am deeply saddened. No matter how Casanova-like he is, a philanderer or seducer, he should never have slept with his own niece, Nneka."

Epilogue

The once ambitious and enthusiastic young Nneka, who had been so desperate and determined to further her education to achieve her full potential, was told to remain in the village of Obodo-Ukwu with her parents after the unanimous decision by the elders and the traditional ruler of the community.

As Nneka's parents could not afford to send her back to school to further her education she remained in her village, helping them with their work on the farm and in the market.

Seven months later Nneka gave birth to a beautiful baby boy. One month later she was distressed when she had to give him to her uncle as had been ordered by the elders and traditional ruler of her community.

Nneka's talents had been wasted, but the devastating seven-year period when she was abused by both her uncle and aunt had come to an end.

Glossary of Nigerian Terms

Nneka	-mother is greater
Oluchi	-the work of God
Ukamaka	-church is good
Ikenna	-God's power
Udoka	-peace
Nwabueze	-child is king
Chimoo	-my God
Nkwo Umunkwo	-community open market

Eze	-traditional ruler
Agbada	-native traditional costume
Obodo Ukwu	-community
Ogbonna	-looks like his father
Umuobom	-a village
Chimoo bia lele	-my God, come and look
Agwuturu mbe	-snake that bites tortoise
Igba Nkwu Nwanui	-traditonal marriage ceremony
Ole	-thief
Onwu na ndu	-death and life
Ngozi	-God's blessing is the best
Naira	-local currency
Nnanyi Onye Eze	-our father the traditional ruler

Printed in Great Britain
by Amazon